Dad Jokes

9 Unique Categories of Groan Producing Jokes, Puns and Riddles

WAIT!!!

READ THIS BEFORE GOING ANY FURTHER!

How would you like to get your next book for FREE and get it before anyone else????

Join our jokester team today and receive your next (and future books) For FREE Signing up is easy and completely free!

Check out this page for more info!!

bit.ly/joketeam

Free Bonus!

Sometimes we all just need a little more laughter in our lives! Experience a variety of top notch jokes with this completely free downloadable book. Sure to put a smile on your face!

Download the free book at:
bit.ly/cmfreebook

Table of Contents

Introduction

I want to thank you for choosing this book, *'Dad Jokes - Top 9 Categories of Hilarious Dad Jokes, Puns and Riddles.'*

One of the defining characteristics that sets us apart from every other animal on the planet is our ability to understand humor and laugh. It is perhaps one of the major aspects of being human that we, as animals, can laugh at certain incidents, things and sometimes people as well. Without humor, human life would have been drab, sad and desolate. It is humor that keeps this world going and thriving.

Imagining a world without humor is not difficult. A world without humor would be a dark and shady place, full of bleak incidents and depressed individuals. But why imagine such a horrifying place when we can enjoy humor?

There are various kinds of humor or methods of making you laugh; however, the most well known method is by telling jokes. Again, there are many kinds of jokes - dark jokes, baby jokes, blonde jokes, non-appropriate jokes, puns, riddles, Little Jonny jokes, holiday jokes etc. Out of these there exists a certain category of jokes that are rarely funny but they still induce groans mixed with laughter. These jokes are known as Dad jokes.

It is a fascinating observation that the concept of dad jokes is universal. Why is it that fathers all around the world make groan-worthy jokes? Is it because the traditional patriarchal outlook of the society does not allow the male parent to showcase their affection towards his progeny in a healthy and unabashed way that makes him utilize bad humor to do so? Or is that all dads are secretly connected and are a part of some big secret society that has a truckload of bad jokes that can embarrass any offspring? We may never know the answer to these questions. However, one thing is quite obvious, we will continue to groan and laugh at dad jokes forever.

This book contains a massive collection of dad jokes that are suitable for all occasions and pretty much all ages. These jokes have been divided into various categories and chapters for the ease of the readers. Furthermore, these chapters are divided into three sections - jokes, puns and riddles, so that you can read them accordingly.

Once again thank you for buying this book and I hope you laugh throughout this book!

Chapter One:

Weirdest - Jokes, Puns and Riddles

Jokes

Son: Dad, did you get a haircut recently?

Dad: *No, I got all of my hair cut recently.*

Question: What is the name of the Mexican who lost his car?

Answer: *Carlos*

Son: Papa, can you put my shoes on?

Father: *No son, they won't fit me.*

Son: (has a test the next day): Dad can I please watch the TV for some time?

Dad: *Yeah, of course son, just don't turn it on.*

I do not recommend eating sushi in this place; *it's very fishy.*

Dad: What would you call a fake noodle?

Son: I don't know dad.

Dad: *An Impasta*

I don't know why people say they pick their nose; I was just born with mine.

Dad: What is sticky and brown?

Son: I don't know that dad, but sounds gross.

Dad: *A stick, of course.*

Hey, did you hear about that new restaurant on the Moon? *Man it has great food but no atmosphere.*

Son: Okay, I'll call you later!

Dad: *Son, please don't do that. Call me dad, I like that better than later.*

Dad: Why did the cookie cry?

Son: Cookies don't cry dad.

Dad: *Because his father was a wafer a long time!*

Son: Dad, help me with this math equation.

Dad: Sure son, what is it?

Son: If 20 men build a house in two months, how much time will 10 men take to build the same house?

Dad: *Nothing. Why do you want to build an already built house?*

What's the son of a mountain climber called?

Cliff.

(Son to his dad while observing a graveyard): **Wow this cemetery is so overcrowded.** *People must be dying to get in here.*

Cashier: Would you like the milk in a bag sir?

Dad: *Um no, leave it in the carton please.*

If I had a dime for each book that I have ever read I'd say, *'Huh, well that's a coincidence."*

I'm never indecisive - *unless you want me to, do you?*

Dad: Son, how many apples grow on a tree?

Son: How would I know that dad?

Dad: *All of them grow on tree son, all of them.*

Son: Dad, please make me a sandwich.

Dad: (Touching the sons head) *Shazam! Here son, you are a sandwich now.*

Did you hear about the new store called Moderation that just opened around the corner? *I hear they have everything there.*

Dad: Son, tell me how can you tell whether an ant is a girl or a boy?

Son: I don't know dad.

Dad: *I'm ashamed son. All of them are girls, if they had been boys; they would be uncles won't they?*

Dad: What cheese can never be your son?

Son: Your cheese?

Dad: *Nacho cheese son.*

To tell the truth, the only thing that is worse than getting diarrhea is having to spell it.

Puns

Want to hear a joke about paper? *Never mind it's tearable.*

Question: How does a penguin construct his house?

Answer: *Igloos it together.*

A steak pun is a rare medium well done.

Question: Why is milk the fastest liquid on earth?

Answer: *It's pasteurized before you can even see it*

I was once employed in a shoe repair shop. *Frankly, it was sole crushing.*

Question: What is a belt with a watch on it known as?

Answer: *A waist of time.*

Question: How do you throw an Outer space themed party?

Answer: *You planet.*

They showed a documentary about beavers last night. *It was definitely the best damn program I have ever watched.*

Riddles

Question: Where will you find a Friday always coming before a Thursday?

Answer: *In a dictionary.*

Question: What has three exits but only one entrance?

Answer: *A T-Shirt*

Question: What rises when rain falls?

Answer: *An Umbrella.*

Question: I know a man who can always tell the exact score of a tennis match even before it begins. How do you think he does that?

Answer: *Anyone can do so as the score before every tennis match is 0:0.*

Question: Which chicken is served but never eaten?

Answer: *A shuttlecock.*

Question: I hear everything but I never speak, who am I?

Answer: *An Ear.*

Chapter Two:

Most Embarrassing -
Jokes, Puns and Riddles

Jokes

Dad: Son, could you please help your brother with this math problem?

Son: Of course, this is a piece of cake dad.

Dad: *No son, this is a math problem, not cake.*

I have been trying to lose weight for a long time *but that damn son of a gun keeps finding me all the time.*

Nah, I am not a big fan of soccer, *I'm here just for the kicks.*

Why do people start doing backflips when they are in love? *Because they are head over heels.*

Dad: Son, why do people never see elephants hiding in trees?

Son: Why?

Dad: *Because they are so good at it!*

10

I heard that two antennae got married recently. *The ceremony was quite boring but the reception was awesome!*

Snowman: Psst!

Snowman2: What?

Snowman: *Do you smell carrots?*

How can you make a tissue dance? *Just wipe your nose and put some boogie in it!*

Son: Why are you staring at the orange juice can dad?

Dad: *It says 'concentrate.'*

Why does your nose run and your feet smell?

I wanted to buy some camouflage trousers last week, *but I didn't find any.*

Sneakers are the best shoes for thieves.

A jumper cable gets into a bar.

Bartender: All right fella, I'll serve ya, *but doncha start nothing.*

Son: How was your experience at the new seafood place last week?

Dad: Oh, it was awful.

Son: Why?

Dad: *I went there and as I sat down, I pulled a mussel.*

Hey did you hear about that guy who stole a calendar. *Apparently he got 12 months.*

The Stock Market: *The only place to buy chicken broth in bulk.*

So what does the ocean say to the shore?

Nothing of course, it just waves.

Son: Dad, what is ET short for?

Dad: *Son, because he has tiny legs.*

Puns

Wow, eating clock is surely time consuming.

Man, Simba was walking so slowly last night *I had to tell him to Mufasa.*

Why do mermaids always wear seashells?

Well because the 'B' shells are too small for them and 'D' ones are too big.

What do sprinters like to eat before an important race?

Nothing really, they fast.

I have always wanted to learn how to drive a stick shift *but I can't ever seem to find a manual.*

I love video games, however I always make puns on them *even when I don't Nintendo.*

What is a fly without wings known as?

A walk.

Why didn't Mama cat allow her kittens to watch the movie last night?

It was from a violent cat-e-gory.

What's a patronizing criminal going down the stairs known as?

A condescending con descending.

What is the difference between Abu Dhabi and Yemen?

People in Yemen do not watch Flintstones *however people in Abu Dhabi doooo.*

Why did no one say anything when the king farted?

It was noble gas.

Two artists got into a competition once.

It ended in a draw.

My sister accidentally stepped on my foot last night. *I had to scream Mitosis to finally get her off.*

What did the Indian kid say to her mum when she left for the party?

Mumbai

I was feeling quite lonely. So I decided to buy some shares. *Now I have a bit of a company.*

Riddles

Question: What has feathers but can't fly?

Answer: *Pillow*

Question: You can sit on it, you can sleep on it and you can brush your teeth with it. What is it?

Answer: *A chair, a bed and a toothbrush.*

Chapter Three:

Dorkiest - Jokes, Puns and Riddles

Dad: What do crabs never give anything to charity?

Son: I don't know dad.

Dad: *Well, because they are shellfish.*

What do you call a Latin man with a rubber toe?

Roberto.

Dad: What do they call a person with no nose and no body either?

Son: What?

Dad: *Nobody nose son, nobody nose.*

I nicked my finger while cutting cheese yesterday, *but now I think I may have a grater problem.*

What is a fish without any eyes called?

Fsh

Dad: What do they call a man with no legs and no arms lying next to your door?

Son: What are you on to dad?

Dad: *They call him 'Matt.'*

My cat was sick on the carpet last night. *I really don't think it is feline well.*

How Are You Enjoying This Book So Far?

I sincerely hope your getting some gut wrenching laughs out of it! I honestly can say I had to stop writing at points because of that. If you have a second I would be so grateful to hear your thoughts about the book! Hearing what my readers have to say makes putting these books together so much more rewarding and gives me drive to do more! It also helps fellow readers make informed purchasing decisions and keeps me being able to do what I love. It only takes a second!

Go Here To Leave A Review On Amazon

bit.ly/atreview

I want to swim in an ocean made of orange soda just once in my life. *It is My Fanta Sea.*

Life without you is like an unsharpened pencil. *Pointless.*

Last night I saw a termite walk into bar. He said, *"Is the bar tender here?"*

Son, I want to give away all my dead batteries today. *Don't worry; it's free of charge.*

Opening an email ID is becoming so pesky now; they want a password with eight characters - *so I picked Snow White and Seven Dwarfs.*

Son: I am afraid of escalators dad, what should I do?

Dad: *Well son, you must start taking some steps to avoid them.*

Son: Why do you want to move to Switzerland all of a sudden? What is the advantage of it?

Dad: *Well son, the flag is definitely a big plus.*

I heard an octopus beat a shark last night in a fight. *Why? It was very well armed.*

Hey did you hear a blue and red ship just collided near the Bermuda. *Apparently, the survivors are all marooned.*

Last night I deleted the contact numbers of all the Germans I know from my phone. Guess what. *It's Hans free now.*

My girlfriend and I watched three movies back to back last night. *Thankfully I was facing the TV.*

What did the Papa spider say to the Kid Spider? *"Stop spending so much time on the web."*

Dad: Son, how much does a hipster weigh?

Son: I don't know.

Dad: *An Instagram.*

Hey did you hear about the new bar that opened up recently. *They have got a band of whales called Orca-stra.*

You should never play cards in a jungle? *Because there are lot of cheetahs in the jungle.*

Why was the feline disqualified from the race? *Because he was a cheetah.*

Dad: Why are bicycles not able to stand on their own?

Son: Because their center of gravity is messed up?

Dad: *No, because they are two tired.*

Puns

My son came to me last night and said, "What rhymes with orange"

I had to tell him off because it does not.

What is the name of that one Chinese billionaire?

Cha Ching.

What will you call a girl with an hourglass figure?

A waist of time.

What food do scientists love?

Fission Chips.

I didn't remember how to throw a boomerang after my accident. *But soon enough, it came back to me.*

The carpenter is quite experienced, *he really nailed it, but this new, inexperienced guy screwed everything up.*

21

What did Mario tell Princess Peach when they broke up?

It's not you; it's a-me, Mario!

What is the difference between a piano and tuna?

You can tuna piano but not piano a tuna.

Why do ballerinas always wear tutus?

Because they can't fit in one-ones and three-threes are quite large.

What jewelries do rabbits love?

Carats.

I wanted to run away with a watermelon after a particularly stormy affair. *But I soon realized that I cantaloupe.*

What animal is the best at baseball?

A bat.

0What did the fish say before hitting a wall?

Oh Dam!

Although I love cake a lot, *I will never dessert you.*

What will you call cows that have a great sense of humor?

Laughing Stock

When is the best time to buy a boat?

When there is a sail on it.

I wanted to catch fog once but *I kept on misting it.*

What did the sea say to the other sea? Nothing, they just WAVED. Oh, don't you SEA what I did there? I'm quite SHORE you did. Come on now; don't be so SALTY? It's quite BEACHY of you.

Roses on piano are the best thing ever.

Nope.

Then?

Tulips on an organ are the best.

How do fish always maintain their weight?

They have their own scales.

I do not like shopping centers, *because once you see one, you've seen a mall.*

Hey, did you know Britney Spears is coming out with a new song?

It's called 'One more Thyme."

I despise stairs. *They are always up to something.*

I will always remember my grandpa's last words before he kicked the bucket. He said," *Hey, how far do you think I can kick this thing?"*

How does an artist make their CV?

He draws on experience.

What is the caretaker of chickens called?

A chicken tender.

Wow, that oyster is quite greedy. *Frankly it is very shellfish.*

Why was 6 scared of 7? *Because 789.*

Why don't people care about the circus?

Because it was quite irr-elephant.

Wow the grapes in the supermarket are really great. *They are really raisin the bars.*

Why couldn't the toilet paper cross the road?

Unfortunately it got stuck in a crack.

I have always wanted to learn how lightning works. *Then at last, it struck me!*

How does a killer get to the forest?

He uses a psychopath.

What did the salad say to tomatoes?

Lettuce be friends.

We cops are quite smart. *Weed know if someone was selling drugs around here.*

Why did Roger quit his job at the donut store? *He was fed up with the hole business.*

Riddles

Question: What has a mouth but never speaks, what has a bed but never rests and what can only run and never walk or jog?

Answer: *A river*

Question: Is the handle of a mug on the left or the right?

Answer: *Neither, it is on the outside.*

Chapter Four:

Worst - Jokes, Puns and Riddles

Jokes

Dad: Why was the Energizer Bunny arrested?

Son: Why?

Dad: *He was charged with battery.*

The perfect recipe for making holy water *is by boiling the hell out of it.*

A sandwich was turned out of a bar last night. *The bartender told him strictly that they don't serve food there.*

Patient: Doctor, I have broken my arm in lots of places.

Doctor: (who is a dad) *Well, you should not go to those places then.*

I am on a strict whiskey diet. *I lost three days already.*

Why did Beau give his pony a glass of water? *The pony was a little horse.*

Dad: Did you hear about that new, revolutionary broom?

Mom: What broom dear?

Dad: *The one that is sweeping the nation?*

My dad always used to say that *atheism is a non-prophet organization.*

I slept like a log last night. Big mistake, *because I woke up in a fireplace next morning.*

Server: Any condiments sir?

Dad: *Compliments? Of course, you look very pretty today.*

Last week I caught two kids playing with a car battery and a firework. *I charged one and let off the other one.*

This new book on the history of glue is great. *I can't seem to put it down.*

Dad: Hey wasn't there a kidnapping at your school?

Son: What!

Dad: *Oh, never mind, he woke up.*

What's a zoo with only one dog call? *A shiatsu*

What did papa tomato tell baby tomato?

Catch up son!

What did baby corn say to mummy corn?

Ma, where is popcorn?

What did the Daddy buffalo say to his kid buffalo when he dropped him off to sleepover?

Bison

What's 50 Cent's name in Kenya?

400 Million Dollars

What would you call a cow with no legs?

Ground beef.

A duck walks into a pharmacy and looks around carefully. He spots a helper and paddles off towards him. The helper looks at the duck and asks: What do you want sir? Duck: I need some chap-stick sonny, *and put it on my bill.*

Why do scarecrows always win awards? *Because they are outstanding in their field.*

My dad once started smearing the road with peanut butter when we were stuck in traffic. *Apparently, peanut butter goes great with jam.*

Why does a chick coop always have two doors? *Because with four doors we would have to call it the chicken sedan.*

Seagulls always avoid going over the bay because *they do not want to be bay-gulls.*

I saw two peanuts walking down the street last night. *One looked like he was a salted.*

Where does Batman go when he needs to poop?

To the batroom

What is the difference between an Indian elephant and an African elephant? *Right about 5000 miles.*

Father: A man went into heavy rain with no umbrella, coat or hat, still his hair did not get wet. How?

Son: No idea

Father: *He was bald*

Son: Dad? Aren't you on a seafood diet?

Dad: Why yes son.

Son: Then why are you eating this cheeseburger?

Dad: *Son, I am on a seafood diet. I see food and I eat it.*

I don't know why the bartender kicked me out last night when I asked him for helicopter flavor chips. *I mean they do make plain chips right?*

Puns

What will you call a Russian tree?

Dimitree

What will you call a Communist Sniper?

A Marxman

Wow, they just fired me from the watch factory even *after all the extra hours I put in.*

What happens when the days end in Bangladesh?

It gets Dhaka.

What kind of tea do capitalists own?

Proper -Tea

Hey, did you check out the new haircut the man on the moon got? *Apparently, Eclipse it himself.*

What did the watch say when it was punched around noon?

It's twelve ow clock.

Why was the photograph sent to prison?

Because it was framed.

What will you call a person who transports cups illegally?

A S-mug-ler

What will you call a bull who is sleeping?

A bulldozer

I entered "How to start a fire" in Google once.

I got 51,000 matches instantly.

Did you read about the guy who was electrocuted?

It was quite shocking!

Riddles

Question: What is the only table you can consume?

Answer: *Vegetable.*

Question: On Thursday, a woman went on horseback for a trip on Friday and then returned after two days on Saturday. How did this happen?

Answer: *The horse was called Friday.*

Chapter Five:

Most over the top -
Jokes, Puns and Riddles

Jokes

Pirate: Arr, the troops be revolting captain!

Captain: *Matey, you be quite repulsive as well.*

Petition to call sheep with no legs *'cloud' is hereby denied.*

Son: How was your dinner last night father?

Dad: *Well son, it was going well until I had seafood. I started feeling a bit eel after.*

Dad: What did 0 say to 8?

Son: What?

Dad: *Nice belt dude.*

Dad: Why do skeletons always seem to be so calm?

Son: I don't know?

Dad: *Because nothing can get under their skin.*

Dad: Another skeleton joke?

Son: No.

Dad: Why do skeletons avoid going on holidays?

Son: Ugh, because they are dead.

Dad: *No, because they have nobody to go with.*

Dad: Why do scuba divers always fall backwards when they go scuba diving?

Son: I don't know, is it some physics jargon?

Dad: *No son, they fall backwards because if they were to fall forwards they would hit the boat.*

There's this new band in town called the Cellophane. *I have heard they do awesome wraps.*

What is the name of magic that cows love to do?

MooDoo

Why do people always invite Superman to lunches?

Because he is a Supperhero.

Oh no, there's something in my shoe?

It is definitely a foot.

Son: Daaaaady, I am hungry!

Dad: *Hello hungry, I am dad.*

If the phone is for me, *don't answer it.*

Son: Dad, what's your best joke?

Dad: *You, my son.*

Son: Where's the bin dad?

Dad: *I haven't been anywhere since a long time.*

Puns

Question: How did the hipster burn her tongue?

Answer: *She tried to drink her coffee before it was too cool.*

Question: Why did that little strawberry cry?

Answer: *Because her mother was caught in a jam.*

Question: Why did the book from the library go to the doctor?

Answer: *It wanted to be checked out.*

Damn, somebody stole my toilet and *now the police have nothing to go on.*

Once in the stadium, I kept wondering why the ball kept getting bigger. *And then it hit me.*

Question: What's a bear with different personalities known as?

Answer: *A bi-polar bear.*

Question: Is the Sun College educated?

Answer: *Yes, it has million degrees.*

My grandpa did not want to become an organ donor so he was buried with all his *musical instruments.*

So, I understand that my ceiling is not the best, *but it is definitely up there.*

Question: Why are mountains so popular?

Answer: *Because they are hill-areas.*

My friend just barged in today and stole milk from my fridge.

How dairy.

Hey did you hear about that new gym that closed down so suddenly?

Yeah, apparently it did not work out.

Where do the sheep go for a haircut?

The baa baa shop.

Did you hear about that escaped fortune telling dwarf?

According to news *a small medium is at large!*

In Australia my puns are thought to be of *high koala-tea.*

Question: What is a steak that tastes bad known as?

Answer: *A Mistake*

Question: Three men are going for a picnic in a boat. Suddenly they decide to have a smoke, but they don't have a lighter or matches. How will they light their cigarettes?

Answer: *They will throw one of the cigarettes overboard which will make the boat lighter.*

Hey, did you know that Iceland is just *a sea away from Ireland?*

Question: Why do cows have hooves instead of regular feet?

Answer: *Because they lactose.*

Question: What will you call a bunch of rabbits walking backwards?

Answer: *A receding hare line.*

Question: What fish is the most popular fish in the ocean?

Answer: *A starfish.*

The furniture store won't stop calling me back. *I made it quite clear the first time that all I wanted was one nightstand.*

Question: What is the difference between a Zippo and a hippo?

Answer: *One is quite heavy while the other one is a lighter.*

Riddles

Question: The only time a person likes being alone is?

Answer: *When he becomes an heir.*

Question: If a doctor gives you 3 pills to take after every half hour, how long will it take you to take all the pills?

Answer: *One hour, you will take the first pill immediately.*

Question: Why the T-Rex can't clap ever?

Answer: *Because they are dead.*

Question: Can a man walk on water?

Answer: *Yes, if the water is really cold.*

Question: If you have 3 apples, 4 pears and 2 bananas in your hand, what do you have?

Answer: *Gigantic hand.*

Question: Tell me a question that cannot be answered with a yes?

Answer: *Are you asleep?*

Question: Another question that cannot be answered with a yes?

Answer: *Are you dead?*

Question: Should a person be allowed to marry the sister of their widow?

Answer: *It does not matter, the man will be dead anyway.*

Question: What has 6 feet [≈ average height of a human] and sings?

Answer: *The singing trio.*

Dad: Which hand do you use to clean your butt?

Son: The right one, why are you asking such an odd question?

Dad: *Oh, I use toilet paper.*

Question: The more holes this thing has, the less it weighs. What is it?

Answer: *Cheese with holes.*

Chapter Six:

Holiday - Jokes, Puns and Riddles

<u>Jokes</u>

Question: What do you call a line of men who are waiting to get a haircut?

Answer: *Barberqueue*

Question: Why do they have a turkey in the pop group?

Answer: *Because he has drumsticks.*

Question: What will you call a boomerang that won't come back?

Answer: *A stick.*

Question: What do snowmen wear on the top of their heads?

Answer: *Ice caps.*

I saw a snowman looking through carrots yesterday. *Fella must have been picking his nose.*

Question: What did Adam say to Eve on the day before Christmas?

Answer: *'It's Christmas Eve!'*

Question: What song does Cinderella sing when her photos do not arrive on time?

Answer: *One day my prints will come!*

Question: Why do vampires like racing?

Answer: *Because it often gets neck to neck.*

Question: What Christmas carol do dogs absolutely love?

Answer: *Bark! The herald angels sing!*

Question: What is Miley Cyrus's favorite food on thanksgivings?

Answer: *Twerky*

Question: What is a snowman's favorite food for breakfast?

Answer: *Snowflakes*

Question: What does Santa do with elves who misbehave?

Answer: *He sacks them.*

Dad: I have the best gift idea for our dear doggie this year.

Son: What is it?

Dad: *A mobile bone!*

Question: Why was Goony the pony gargling?

Answer: *It was a little horse.*

Dad: Why can't Christmas trees ever finish their knitting?

Son: Why?

Dad: *Because they keep on dropping their needles.*

Question: Why does Father Christmas send his elves to school?

Answer: *To learn the elf-abet.*

Question: What TV show do horses love?

Answer: *Neighbors*

Question: What TV show does Santa love?

Answer: *Sleighbors*

Question: What TV show does Hercules love?

Answer: *Labors*

Question: What would you call a train that is loaded with toffee?

Answer: *A chew-chew train*

Question: Why do skeletons do not like going to parties?

Answer: *Because they have no body to go with.*

Question: Why doesn't Father Christmas give away Rudolph and Blitzen?

Answer: *Because they are two deer to him.*

Question: What is a snowman's favorite way of getting around?

Answer: *They love 'icicles.*

Question: What is a snowman's favorite way of getting around?

Answer: *Are you daft, snowman can't move.*

Question: Who hides in bakeries around holidays?

Answer: *A mince spy.*

Dad: Son, I have got a present for you that you cannot beat!

Son: Oh my God! What is it?

Dad: *A broken drum!*

I have a friend who loves standing between two goal posts.
Her name is Annette.

Question: What has four legs but cannot walk?

Answer: *A chair.*

Question: Who says 'Oh, Oh, Oh?'

Answer: *Santa going backwards.*

Question: Why did Father Christmas go to the hospital last night?

Answer: *Oh it is because of his poor elf.*

Question: What is a frogs' favorite footwear?

Answer: *Open toad sandals.*

Son: Why are pirates called pirates dad?

Dad: *Son, because they arrrrrrr!*

Dad: Hey son, what do they call a blind reindeer?

Son: I don't know dad, what do they call it?

Dad: *No eye deer.*

Question: What's bad tempered and round?

Answer: *A vicious circle.*

Question: How can you tell if Santa's been in your garden shed?

Answer: You will have three extra hoes.

Question: What's yellow and extremely deadly?

Answer: *Shark-infested custard.*

It gets quite cold in St. Petersburg in winters with a lot of snowfall and rain. On one such night in winter, a Russian couple was walking down a busy street in the city when the man felt something hit his nose gently. 'Oh my, I think it is raining!' he exclaimed to his wife.

"I don't think so dear, that was definitely snow, it did look like snow to me," she said. "No, no dear, I am sure it was rain, I felt it on my nose," he replied. And soon they got into a huge argument over whether it was snow or just rain. They notice a small time official walking by them when the husband said, "Let us quit fighting dear and find out by asking Comrade Rudolph if it was really snowing or raining."

The woman agreed and they approached the comrade. "Comrade Rudolph! Tell us whether it was snowing or raining just now?"

"Why, of course, it's raining!" the officer answered and moved on. Quite satisfied with the answer the man started to walk as well however the woman was still unhappy. She said, 'I am still sure that it was snow and not rain. The man came back and said *"Listen, Rudolph the Red knows rain, dear."*

Dad: How is Christmas similar to a cat lost in the Sahara?

Son: I don't know?

Dad: *Both have sandy claws.*

Dad: What's the best time for Santa to go down a chimney?

Son: What?

Dad: *Anytime of course.*

Dad: Knock, knock.

Son: Who's there?

Dad: Pizza.

Son: Pizza, who?

Dad: *Pizza on earth, good will toward men!*

Dad: What stories do birds absolutely love?

Son: I am not sure.

Dad: *The Finch Who Stole Christmas.*

Dad: Hey did you know about that shark that gives away gifts on Christmas?

Son: What?

Dad: *Yeah, it's called Santa Jaws.*

Son: What are you giving Papa for holidays?

Mother: *Oh, just a list of everything I want dear!*

Dad: Say son what do you think snowmen do on the weekend?

Son: I don't know.

Dad: *They just chill out.*

Dad: What is Jack Frost's favorite thing about school?

Son: What?

Dad: *Snow and tell.*

Dad: What will you get if you cross an iPhone with a Christmas tree?

Son: What?

Dad: *A pineapple!*

Dad: What do you plan to give your little brother these holidays?

Son: Well I am not sure yet.

Dad: What did you give him last year?

Son: *The measles.*

Dad: Who loves children, brings them gifts and then scratches the furniture?

Son: I don't know?

Dad: *Santa Claws.*

Dad: What does the road service use in the North Pole?

Son: I am not sure?

Dad: *Snow cones!*

Dad: What elections do polar bears vote in?

Son: What?

Dad: *The North Poll!*

Dad: Son, what is the definition of claustrophobia?

Son: The fear of closed spaces?

Dad: *No son, it is the fear of Santa Claus.*

Dad: Say what do you elves do after their school?

Son: I don't know.

Dad: *Their gnome work!*

Dad: What is the nationality of Father Christmas?

Son: What?

Dad: *North Polish.*

Dad: What's the difference between a knight and Father Christmas's reindeer?

Son: I don't know.

Dad: *One slays the dragon, and the other is always draggin' the sleigh.*

Dad: I have been wondering son.

Son: Wondering what dad?

Dad: *Does Santa Claus refer to his elves as 'subordinate clauses'?*

Dad: Knock knock!

Son: Who's there?

Dad: Dexter

Son: Dexter, who?

Dad: *Dexter hall with boughs of holly.*

Dad: Son, what will you get if you try to cross a dog and a snowman?

Son: No.

Dad: *Frostbite.*

Dad: How does Santa open a race?

Son: I don't know.

Dad: *Ready, set, Ho! Ho! Ho!*

Dad: Hey did you hear Santa's little helper's been seeing a shrink nowadays?

Son: What? Why?

Dad: *Because apparently, he had low elf esteem!*

Dad: What did Rudolph say to the soccer player?

Son: I don't know.

Dad: *Your Blitzen days are over!*

Dad: How do sheep say "Merry Christmas"?

Son: How?

Dad: *Fleece Navidad.*

<u>Puns</u>

Hey, what kind of jeans would you love? - *Holy jeans*

I bought a new fridge for my daughter this Thanksgiving.
I can't wait to see her face light up when she finally opens it.

Question: Where do you think Noah kept his bees?

Answer: *In the ark hives.*

Question: What will you call a fruit that argues against the position that it likes?

Answer: *The devil's advocado.*

Dad: Why did not Jesus buy beer? *Because Hebrew it.*

Chapter Seven:

Everyday - Jokes, Puns and Riddles

Jokes

Dad: What time did my fried Jim go to the dentist?

Son: How would I know that?

Dad: *Tooth hurt-y*

Dad: Hey, I am reading a great book on anti-gravity!

Son: Wow, how is it?

Dad: *It's frankly impossible to put down!*

Dad: You are Australian when you go in the washroom, and when you come out, you are Australian as well. But what are you when you are in the washroom?

Son: Australian?

Dad: *European*

Dad: Son, I saw a robbery at the Apple Store down the corner.

Son: Oh!

Dad: *Yes, I am an iWitness now.*

Dad: Oh my God, spring is here! I am so happy! I am so excited that I seem to have wet my plants!

Dad: What is Forrest Gump's password?

Son: What?

Dad: *1forrest1*

Dad: Hey did you hear about that woman who invented in Lifesavers?

Son: Why, what happened?

Dad: *Apparently she made a mint.*

Dad: I bought this pair of shoes from a drug dealer. I really don't know what he laced them with but I have been tripping throughout the day.

Dad: What do you call a factory that makes passable objects?

Son: I don't know.

Dad: *A satisfactory.*

Son: I was thinking dad that...

Dad: *Oh, so that's where this weird burning smell is coming from!*

Dad: Why did the invisible man decline the job offer?

Son: Why?

Dad: *He could not see him doing it.*

Dad: You know I worked at a calendar factory once upon a time.

Son: Oh, really? What happened?

Dad: *They fired me because I took a few days off.*

Once a woman was put on trial for beating her husband to death with his guitars. The judge said "First offender?" She replied, *"No, first it was a Gibson and later a Fender."*

Dad: What did the three-legged dog say to the bartender?

Son: Bow-wow

Dad: *I am looking for the guy who shot my paw.*

Son: Are you all right dad?

Dad: *No son, I'm half left as well.*

Mall Clerk: Plastic or paper?

Dad: *Oh, anything will do, you see I am bisacktual.*

Puns

Question: What will you call an escaped convict who happens to be a vegetable?

Answer: *An escapea.*

I love 06:30. *It is hands down the best time on a clock.*

I really do not like how almost all funerals start early in the day. *I am not a mourning person you know.*

I cleaned my space rack today. However, everything was quite old and I had to throw it out. *It was quite a waste of thyme.*

Question: What will you ask you sister if you see her crying?

Answer: *Are you having a crisis?*

Question: Will glass coffins be successful?

Answer: *Well, remains to be seen.*

Hey did you hear about that guy who was buried alive?
Yeah, a grave mistake indeed.

Question: How can you cut Rome in two?

Answer: *With a pair of Caesars.*

Okay, I cannot spell Armageddon. *But it is not the end of the world so chill.*

Two windmills were standing next to each other awkwardly. One of them asked, in the hope of breaking the ice, 'What music do you listen to?' The other replied, 'Oh, I am a *huge metal fan."*

Question: Why do they call the Middle Ages the Dark Ages?

Answer: *Because they had too many knights.*

Question: What will you call 2 octopuses who look exactly alike?

Answer: *Itenticle*

What do you call 2 octopuses that look exactly the same? – *Itenticle.*

Question: Why was the tomato blushing?

Answer: *It saw the salad dressing.*

An atom loses an electron… It says, *"Man, I really gotta keep an ion them."*

My friend is lagging behind on paying his water bill and he may lose the connection, *so I sent him a card saying, "Get well soon."*

Question: What will you call a cow who jumped over the barbed wire?

Answer: *Udder destruction*

I heard someone was killed last night with a starter pistol. *I heard them saying that it was probably race related.*

Riddles

Question: Who suffers the most from the yo-yo effect?

Answer: *The moon. It loses and gains every month.*

Question: Which nails are extremely painful to hammer in?

Answer: *Your fingernails.*

Question: Which animal turns around 200 times on its axis after passing away?

Answer: *A roast chicken.*

Question: Which lion can swim very well?

Answer: *The sea lion.*

Question: What question can only be answered with Yes?

Answer: *How do you spell the word Yes?*

Question: How many months have 28 days?

Answer: *All of them have 28 days.*

Chapter Eight:

Most Random Jokes, Puns and Riddles

Dad: How can you differentiate between a horny toad and a frog?

Son: I don't know, their color maybe?

Dad: *A frog goes 'Ribbit, ribbit' and a horny toad goes 'Rub it, rub it.'*

Dad: Hey did you know that FedEx and UPS are merging.

Son: No, not really

Dad: *Yeah, they are going to go by the name Fed-Up now.*

Do you know about 10/8 people agree that they are quite bad at fractions.

Mom: Hey honey, how do I look?

Dad: *With you eyes dear, with your eyes.*

Dad: What fruit does Beethoven love?

Son: I don't know.

Dad: *A ba na na na.*

Dad: What was the first thing that the horse says after tripping?

Son: Neigh?

Dad: *No. Help, I can't giddy up!*

I saw two guys walk in the bar. *The third ducked though. Smart chap.*

Question: What will you call a masturbating cow?

Answer: *Beef Stroganoff.*

Dad: Hey did you hear about that crazy fire in the circus?

Son: No?

Dad: *Yeah, it was very in tents!*

Dad: Son never trust atoms.

Son: Why?

Dad: *Well they make up everything!*

Dad: What will you call a cow that has only two legs?

Son: I don't know.

Dad: *Lean beef*

Son: Ugh dad.

Dad: Okay now what will you call a cow with no legs?

Son: What?

Dad: *Ground beef.*

Dad: What will you call the cross of a rhino and elephant?

Son: What?

Dad: *Elephino.*

Dad: How can you make an octopus laugh?

Son: I don't know?

Dad: *You can ten-tickle it.*

Dad: I only know 25 letters of the English alphabet.

Son: What?

Dad: *Yeah, I don't know why.*

Dad and son are walking around the corner when suddenly an ambulance zips past them, *blaring its siren loudly.*

Dad: *Wow, they sure won't sell any ice cream if they keep on driving at that pace.*

Dad: Why are cows always so great at their job?

Son: Why?

Dad: *Because they are out standing in their fields.*

Dad: What is the name of that famous dog magician?

Son: I don't know.

Dad: *Labracadabrador.*

Puns

I want to marry a pencil now. I really can't wait for my folks to meet *my bride 2B.*

Question: Why did coffee register a police report?

Answer: *Because someone mugged it.*

Last week I went to a job interview where the manager said that they were looking for responsible people. I told him I was his man *because I was held responsible for everything that went wrong at my last job.* I did not get the new job.

Rest in peace, boiling water. *I will mist you!*

I sued the airport for losing my luggage, *but I lost my case.*

Honestly, my excessively poor knowledge of Greek mythology will always be my Achilles' elbow.

What did the shore say when the tide arrived?

Long time, no sea.

Let me tell you, if trees could kill, *they wood kill you.*

Riddles

Question: Who earns a livelihood without working a single day?

Answer: *The night watchman.*

Question: Who can smell without a nose?

Answer: *The cheese.*

Question: Who has an extremely exhausting life?

Answer: *The exhaust pipe.*

Question: What always goes swimming with you but never comes out wet?

Answer: *Your shadow.*

Question: What is the most significant difference between toilet paper and a car?

Answer: *You can buy a used car.*

Chapter Nine:

Most Typical - Jokes, Puns and Riddles

Jokes

Dad: Why do cannibals not eat clowns?

Son: Why don't you tell me dad?

Dad: *Clowns taste funny*

Waitress: Soup or salad sir?

Dad: *I don't want a super salad miss; just give me the regular one.*

Dad: Why will no vampire ever attack Taylor Swift?

Son: I don't know?

Dad: *Because she's got Bad Blood.*

Dad: You know prisoners can make calls now?

Son: Oh, how?

Dad: *Using cell phones.*

Hey, do you know about the fattest knight at the Round Table. He was called Sir Cumference *and apparently he got too fat from too much pi.*

Dad: They made round bails of hay illegal last night.

Son: What, why?

Dad: *They thought the cows were not having proper square meals.*

Nurse: Blood type sir?

Dad: *Red of course.*

Waiter: Sorry about the wait sir.

Dad: *Excuse me; are you calling me fat?*

Dad: What will call a fish with two knees?

Son: I don't know?

Dad: *A two-knee fish.*

Dad: Do you know what happened to the man who tried to feed a bear an Apple?

Son: What?

Dad: *His action did not bear fruit*

The loudest pet you can every get *is always and ever a trumpet.*

I was charged and interrogated me over the theft of a sandwich. *Man, the way they grilled was rough.*

Hey, can February March? *Not really, but April May.*

Dad: Which cheese is the loneliest of all the cheese?

Son: Bad cheese?

Dad: *Provolone*

Dad: Why has not anyone ever heard a pterodactyl go to a bathroom?

Son: Why?

Dad: *Because the pee is not pronounced.*

Dad: What kind of meals do math teachers love to eat?

Son: Tasty ones?

Answer: *No silly, Square Meals*

Dad: What's the staple food of a vegan zombie?

Son: What?

Dad: *GRAAAAAAINS*

Dad: What does an angry chilly do?

Son: What?

Dad: *It is jalapeno your face.*

Dad: Why wasn't your mom happy with the Velcro shoe she bought yesterday?

Son: It did not fit her?

Dad: *No, it was a total rip-off.*

Dad: Where will Edward from Twilight for shopping?

Son: Where?

Dad: *Forever 21*

Dad: Hey did you hear about that crazy new band called 1023 MB?

Son: No?

Dad: *Yeah, they are great but they have got no gig yet.*

Dad: Hey son, good luck for your auditions. And don't forget to take a bucket!

Son: Thanks dad, but bucket? Why?

Dad: *Oh, so that you can carry your tune of course!*

Puns

Question: How did the man lose his job at the bank on his very first day?

Answer: *A customer asked him to check her balance, so he pushed her.*

Question: How do trees use Internet?

Answer: *They log in.*

The future, the present and the past walked into a bar last night.

The situation was quite tense.

According to a great philosopher, if a man runs behind a car will get exhausted, however, if a man runs in front of a car, *he will get tired.*

Riddles

Question: Let us assume that you have 20 apples in a basket. Now you have 20 hungry people who need to be fed. You can give an apple to each person; however, one apple should remain in the basket. How will you do this?

Answer: *First you distribute 19 apples among 19 people and then give the last person the basket containing the apple.*

Question: Why don't keyboards sleep?

Answer: They have two shifts

Question: What is at the center of Earth?

Answer: *R. (The center of the word 'Earth' is 'R'.)*

Question: Who can eat a lot of iron without getting sick ever?

Answer: *The rust.*

Question: If the child is going to school for the first time, where will she sit?

Answer: *Nowhere, she is still going to the school.*

Question: How much earth will be there in a 3x3 feet deep hole?

Answer: *Nothing. If it's a hole, there will be no earth in it.*

Question: Why can ghosts never lie to you?

Answer: *You can see right through them!*

Conclusion

I want to personally thank you for buying this book! I sincerely hope you got some good eye watering laughs out of it! I can't tell you how many times I did in the process of putting it together!

Dad jokes, though often groan-worthy, are still quite enjoyable and hilarious. They are often extremely bad and it is strange that we still like them. Maybe it's our love and adoration towards our fathers that allows us to enjoy such bad jokes. Maybe we just can't help but laugh at how bad they are. I think we can agree that they do have a sense of cleverness to them. I hope this book was a good trip into nostalgia for people who have grown up with dad jokes. I really enjoyed putting it together and I hope you got a lot of value from it.

If its okay I'd like to ask you for a favour. Reviews are the lifeblood of my books and I would be over the top grateful to hear your thoughts about it! This will help me in the creation of making future books and will help fellow readers make an informed purchasing decision. I love hearing what my readers have to say about my books and it makes it so much more rewarding! I would love to hear from you! Thank you I appreciate your time and feedback!

Go Here To Leave A Review On Amazon

bit.ly/atreview

WAIT!!!

READ THIS BEFORE GOING ANY FURTHER!

How would you like to get your next book for FREE and get it before anyone else????

Join our jokester team today and receive your next (and future books) For FREE Signing up is easy and completely free!

Check out this page for more info!!

bit.ly/joketeam

Free Bonus!

Sometimes we all just need a little more laughter in our

lives! Experience a variety of top notch jokes with this

completely free downloadable book. Sure to put a smile on

your face!

Download the free book at:

bit.ly/cmfreebook

Resources

https://www.buzzfeed.com/amphtml/mikespohr/29-dad-jokes-that-are-so-bad-their-actually-good

http://pun.me/pages/dad-jokes.php

https://www.popsugar.com/moms/Best-Dad-Jokes-All-Time-38747651/amp

http://twentytwowords.com/the-biggest-collection-of-dad-jokes-youve-ever

https://www.buzzfeed.com/keelyflaherty/jokes-you-can-out-dad-your-dad-with-this-christmas?utm_term=.vhaBB-WZ7L#.gpQaadng7

http://www.laughfactory.com/jokes/holiday-jokes

http://www.short-funny.com/funny-riddles-answers.php

Made in the USA
Monee, IL
29 October 2023